MW01434196

Nita Mehta's
Indian LOW FAT cookbook

Vegetarian

Nita Mehta

B.Sc. (Home Science), M.Sc. (Food and Nutrition), Gold Medalist

Tanya Mehta

SNAB
Publishers Pvt Ltd

Nita Mehta's
Indian LOW FAT cookbook

© Copyright 2003 **SNAB** Publishers Pvt Ltd

WORLD RIGHTS RESERVED. The contents—all recipes, photographs and drawings are original and copyrighted. No portion of this book shall be reproduced, stored in a retrieval system or transmitted by any means, electronic, mechanical, photocopying, recording or otherwise, without the written permission of the publishers.

While every precaution is taken in the preparation of this book, the publisher and the author assume no responsibility for errors or omissions. Neither is any liability assumed for damages resulting from the use of information contained herein.

TRADEMARKS ACKNOWLEDGED. Trademarks used, if any, are acknowledged as trademarks of their respective owners. These are used as reference only and no trademark infringement is intended upon.

First Edition 2003
ISBN 81-7869-055-1

Food Styling and Photography: **SNAB**

Layout and laser typesetting :

National Information Technology Academy
3A/3, Asaf Ali Road
New Delhi-110002
N.I.T.A. ☎ 23252948

Published by :
SNAB Publishers Pvt. Ltd.
3A/3 Asaf Ali Road,
New Delhi - 110002
Tel: 23252948, 23250091
Telefax: 91-11-23250091

Editorial and Marketing office:
E-348, Greater Kailash-II, N.Delhi-48
Fax: 91-11-26235218 Tel: 91-11-26214011, 26238727
E-Mail: nitamehta@email.com
snab@snabindia.com
Website: http://www.nitamehta.com
Website: http://www.snabindia.com

Distributed by :
THE VARIETY BOOK DEPOT
A.V.G. Bhavan, M 3 Con Circus,
New Delhi - 110 001
Tel: 23417175, 23412567; Fax: 23415335

Printed by :
INTERNATIONAL PRINT-O-PAC LIMITED

Rs. 89/-

ೞ✣ೞ

Picture on cover:	*Mili Juli Subzi*	*Recipe on page 52*
Picture on page 1:	*Kandhari Kebab*	*Recipe on page 12*
Picture on inside front cover:	Kashmiri Khumb Matar	Recipe on page 32
Picture on page 2:	*Dal Makhani*	*Recipe on page 50*
	Haryali Paneer Tikka	*............... 16*
Picture on back cover:	*Saunfiyan Tori Tukri*	*Recipe on page 62*

ೞ✣ೞ

Introduction

Yes, now Indian food can be low fat and low calorie. No more boring boiled food or salads when on a diet; the low cal Indian recipes created here will fit easily into your life style! Cooked carefully with the right blend of spices, all vegetables can be made delicious, even if the fat is cut to the minimum.

Delicious curries made in a teaspoon of oil using boiled onion paste and yogurt are here to surprise you. The snacks are all steamed or grilled. A few panfried snacks using a teaspoon of oil will satisfy your craving for fried food. The oven, which is the new invention for the Indian tandoor brings out some fascinating quick dishes which will be relished by the Indian palates. The Indian delicacies like kebabs and tikkas are all made the low fat way. And when you are on a low fat diet, you need not completely stay away from desserts. Kulfi made with paneer instead of khoya, rabri with low fat milk and khubanis in kewra syrup will satisfy the sweet tooth without guilt!

There is no need to starve yourself to look good. This cookbook will help you remain slim, healthy and beautiful.

Nita Mehta

Indian LOW FAT

About The Recipes
What's in a cup?

INDIAN CUP
1 teacup = 200 ml liquid
AMERICAN CUP
1 cup = 240 ml liquid (8 oz.)

The recipes in this book were tested with the Indian teacup which holds 200 ml liquid.

CONTENTS

Introduction 6

Snacks & Starters 10

Suji waale Toast 11	Bharwaan Khandavi 18
Kandhari Kebabs 12	Kebab Hara Bhara 22
Baked Yogurt Wheels 14	Subz Chokker Tikki 24
Haryali Paneer Tikka 16	Cornflakes ki Chaat 25
	Paalak Idlis 26

Curries & Wet Dishes   28

Palak Paneer   29
Kandhari Aloo   30
Kashmiri Khumb Matar   32
Mixed Vegetable Curry   34
Saunfiyaan Dhania Paneer   36
Baked Kofta Curry   40
Chana & Nugget Curry   42
Paneer Makhani   44
Water Melon Curry   46
Dal Makhani (without makhan)   50

Dry & Semidry Dishes   51

Mili Juli Subzi   52
Sambhari Bhindi   54
Nugget Keema   55
Khatti Mithi Subzi   56
Cabbage Pea Poriyal   60
Saunfiyan Tori Tukri   62
Hara Pyaz Khumb   64
Safed Jalpari   66
Moong Stuffed Tinda   70
Saunf-Imli Waale Baingan   72
Pao Bhaji Masala Gobi   74
Kastoori Gajar Matar   76
Bread Dahi Badas   78
Broccoli Achaari   80
Phalli Tamatar Kairi   82

From the Oven 83

Kabuli Chana Bake 84
Tandoori Paneer ki Subzi 88
Jeera Khumb with Baingan 90
Indian Chana Pizza 92

Low Calorie Desserts 94

Phirni 94
Stuffed Khubani in Syrup 96
Orange Rabri 99
Seb (Apple) ka Meetha 100
Chenna Kulfi 102

Snacks & Starters

Indian LOW FAT

Suji Waale Toast

cal/portion 27   *Serves* 6

2 tbsp suji (semolina), ½ tsp rai (small brown mustard seeds)
75 gm paneer - crumbled (¾ cup)
½ tsp salt, or to taste, ¼ tsp pepper, or to taste
½ onion - very finely chopped, 2 tbsp curry leaves
½ tomato - cut into half, deseeded and chopped finely
3 bread slices - toasted in a toaster
3 tsp oil to shallow fry

1. Mix paneer with suji, salt & pepper. Add onion, tomato & curry leaves.
2. Spread paneer mixture carefully on toasted bread, keeping edges neat.
3. Sprinkle some rai over the paneer mixture, pressing down gently.
4. Heat 1 tsp oil in a non stick pan. Add a slice of bread with topping side down. Cook until the topping turns golden brown and crisp.
5. Add a little more oil for the next slice if required. Cut each slice into 4 pieces and serve hot.

Kandhari Kebabs

Picture on page 1 *Serves 8* *cal/portion 75*

¼ cup anaar ke dane, 1 tbsp oil, 3 tbsp thick curd, approx.

BOIL TOGETHER
1 cup kale channe, ½ cup channe ki dal (split gram)

ADD TO GROUND CHANA MIX
2 green chillies - chopped finely
2 onions - chopped finely
1" piece ginger and 4-5 flakes garlic - crushed or 1 tbsp ginger-garlic paste
1¼ tsp salt, ½ tsp garam masala, ½ tsp amchoor (dried mango powder)

CRUSH TOGETHER
¼ tsp jeera (cumin seeds), seeds of 2 moti illaichi (brown cardamoms)
3-4 laung (cloves) - crushed, 3-4 saboot kali mirch (peppercorns)

BASTING (POURING ON KEBABS)
3 tbsp milk

Indian LOW FAT

1. Soak chaane ki dal and kale chaane in some water for 1 hour. Drain water. Pressure cook Chanas and dal with 1½ cups water. After the first whistle, keep cooker on slow fire for 15 minutes. Remove from fire.
2. After the pressure drops down, strain Chanas. Discard water.
3. Divide boiled Chana mixture into 2 portions. Grind one portion in a grinder just for few seconds. Do not make it a smooth paste. Let it be rough. Grind the left over Chanas also in the same way. Mix all together. (Grinding small quantities of Chana at one time is better).
4. Add green chillies, onions, salt, ginger, garlic, garam masala and amchoor to Chana paste.
5. Crush jeera, moti illaichi, laung, saboot kali mirch and mix.
6. Heat 1 tbsp oil in pan, add Chana mixture. Cook for 3- 4 minutes.
7. Remove from fire. Add anaar ke daane. Mix well. Add curd to bind the mixture properly.
8. Check salt and add more salt, if required. Make small round discs.
9. Grill at 230°C for about 10 minutes. Baste (brush) some milk on each kebabs to keep them moist. Grill again for 10 minutes or till done. Serve hot with mint chutney.

Baked Yogurt Wheels

Serves 4 *cal/portion 36*

4 slices of soft fresh bread, 2-3 tbsp milk, 1 tsp ajwain (carom seeds)
4 tbsp moong sprouts, optional
9 paalak (spinach) leaves

FILLING

1 cup curd - hang for 1 hour in a thin muslin cloth and squeeze
½ carrot - grated (½ cup) & squeezed, 1 capsicum - finely chopped (½ cup)
1 green chilli - deseeded & finely chopped
1 tsp salt, ½ tsp crushed peppercorns, ¼ tsp each dhania & red chilli powder
1 tsp tomato ketchup (masala chilli), ½ tsp bhuna jeera powder

1. Hang curd for 1 hour. Squeeze well to drain out all water. Put the curd in a bowl. Add all other ingredients of the filling to the curd and mix lightly with a fork. Keep filling aside.
2. Cut the sides of a slice, keep it flat on a rolling board.

Indian LOW FAT

3. Press, applying pressure with a belan so that holes of the bread close. Keep aside. Similarly roll another slice. (You may microwave the bread slice for a few seconds before rolling.)
4. Keep both the slices slightly overlapping, about ¼" to get a long piece.
5. Press with belan on the joint. Spread spinach leaves (cut stalks completely) on bread.
6. Spread a layer of filling on leaf & empty spaces
7. Sprinkle ajwain on the fillling. Sprinkle some sprouts. Roll carefully.
8. Seal end by applying some curd. Press well.
9. Brush milk on roll. Spread some ajwain on a plate and roll the bread roll over it. Gently cut each roll into 4-5 pieces to get wheels of about ¾" thickness.
10. At serving time, cover a wire rack of oven with foil. Grease foil lightly. Place wheels standing upright on it. Bake in a hot oven (200°C) for about 10 minutes till edges turn golden. Serve immediately.

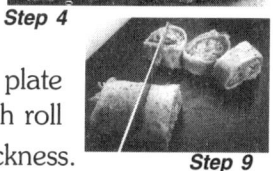

Haryali Paneer Tikka

Paneer tikka coated with fennel flavoured green chutney.

Picture on page 2 *Serves 6-8* *cal/portion 45*

400 gm paneer - cut into 1½" long pieces, ¾" thick
4 tbsp besan (gram flour)
1 tsp salt, 1 tsp oil

GRIND TO A FINE PASTE (CHUTNEY)
1 cup fresh green dhania (green coriander)
1 green chilli, 2 tsp saunf (fennel)
5-6 flakes garlic, 1" piece ginger
4 tbsp lemon juice
½ tsp salt

1. Grind together dhania, green chilli, saunf, ginger, garlic, lemon juice and salt to a fine paste.
2. Slit paneer pieces almost till the end, keeping the end intact. Keep aside.

Indian LOW FAT

3. Divide the chutney into 2 parts.
4. With one part of the chutney, stuff some chutney in the slits of all the paneer pieces. Keep the stuffed paneer aside.
5. To the left over chutney, add 4 tbsp besan and 1 tsp salt. Rub this paste all over the stuffed paneer pieces.
6. Rub some oil over the grill of the oven or wire rack of a gas tandoor. Place paneer on the greased wire rack or grill of the oven.
7. Heat an oven to 180°C or a gas tandoor on moderate flame. Grill paneer for 15 minutes. Spoon some drops of oil or melted butter on the paneer pieces in the oven or tandoor and grill further for 5 minutes. Serve hot.

Note:
- To cook the tikkas in the oven, place an aluminium tray covered with aluminium foil under the wire rack on which the tikkas are placed, to collect the drippings. This makes cleaning simpler.
- While skewering or placing the tikka on the grill, the pieces should be arranged such that there is atleast 1" gap between them so that each piece can get it's own space and heat all around to get cooked properly.

Bharwaan Khandavi

A very popular snack of Western India. Strips of cooked gram flour are rolled into a delicious snack. The filling makes all the difference.

Picture on facing page   Serves 8   *cal/portion 35*

½ cup besan (gram flour)
½ cup curd (not sour) mixed with 1 cup water to get 1½ cups butter milk (lassi)
¼ tsp haldi (turmeric powder), ¼ tsp jeera powder (ground cumin seeds)
½ tsp dhania powder, a pinch of hing (asafoetida) powder, 1 tsp salt
½" piece ginger and 1-2 green chillies - grind to a paste together

FILLING

½ tbsp oil, ½ tsp rai, 1 tsp kishmish - chopped, 1 tbsp chopped coriander
2 tbsp grated carrot, 1 tbsp grated fresh coconut, 2 pinches salt

CHOWNK (TEMPERING)

½ tbsp oil, ½ tsp rai (small, brown mustard seeds)
2-3 green chillies - cut into thin long pieces, a few coriander leaves

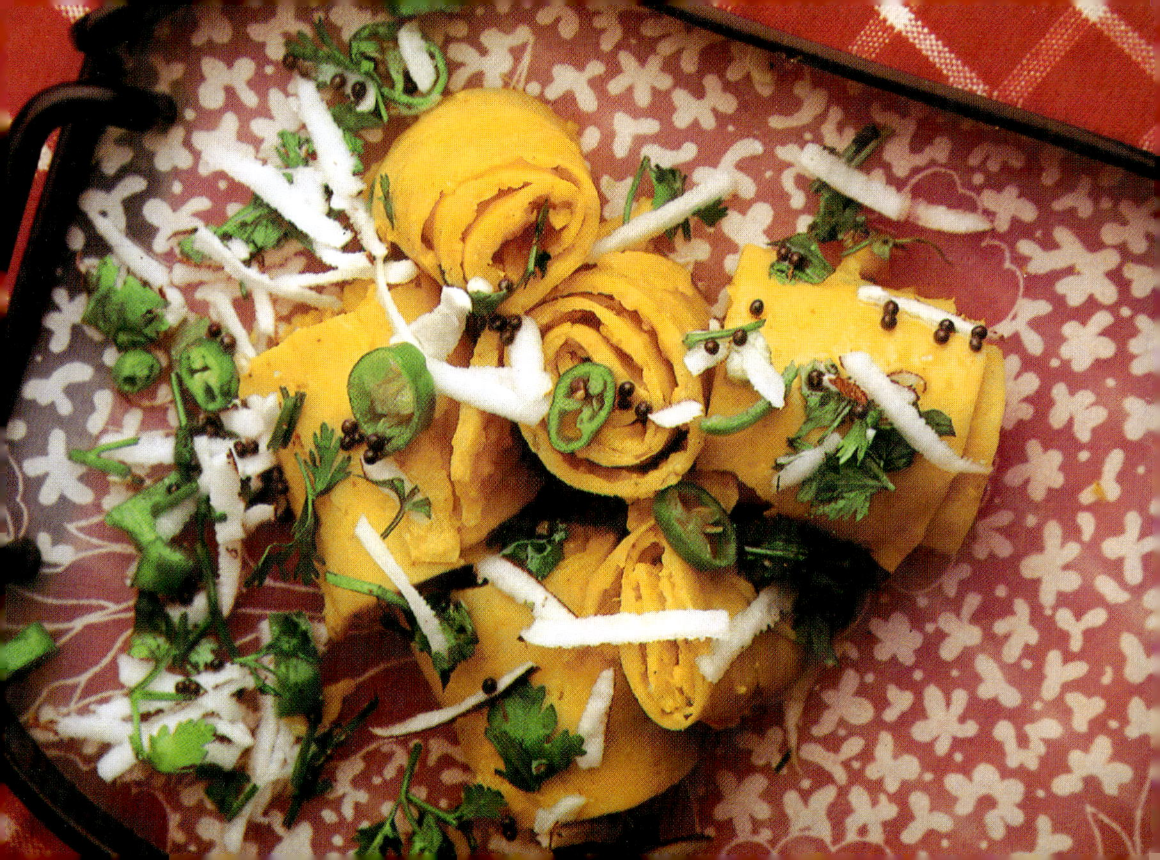

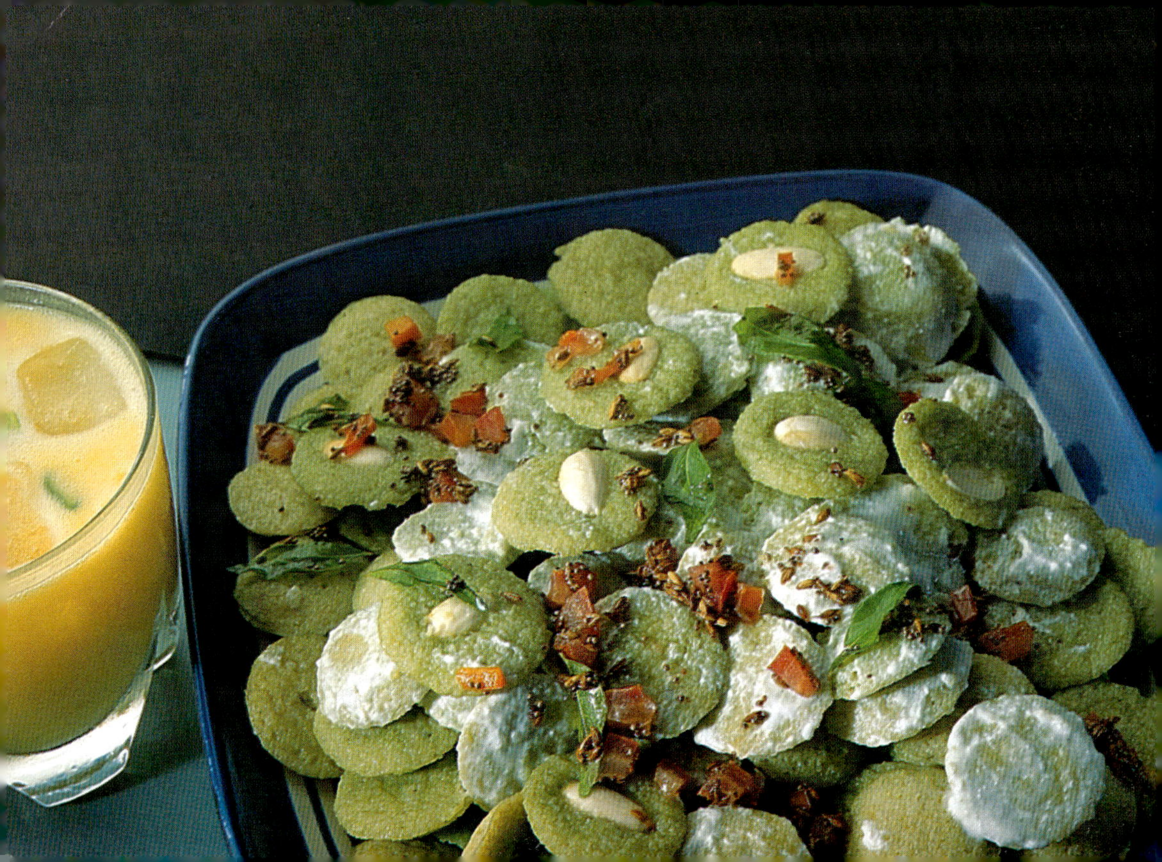

Indian LOW FAT

1. Mix besan with 1½ cups buttermilk till smooth. Add haldi, jeera powder, dhania powder, hing, salt and ginger-green chilli paste.
2. Spread a cling film (plastic sheet) on the backside of a big tray.
3. Keep the mixture on low heat in a non stick pan. Cook this mixture for about 25 minutes, stirring, till the mixture becomes very thick and translucent. Drop 1 tsp mixture on the tray and spread. Let it cool for a while and check if it comes out easily. If it does, remove from fire, otherwise cook for another 5 minutes. Remove from fire.
4. While the mixture is still hot, quickly spread some mixture as thinly & evenly as possible on the cling film. Level it with a knife. Keep aside.
5. For the filling, heat oil. Add rai. After it crackles, add coconut, carrot, kishmish and chopped coriander. Add salt. Mix. Remove from fire.
6. After the besan mixture cools, neaten the rectangle by cutting the edges straight with a knife. Cut widthwise into 2" wide strips.
7. Put 1 tsp filling at one end of a strip. Roll each strip, loosening with a knife initially, to get small cylinders. Keep in a serving plate.
8. Heat ½ tbsp oil. Add rai. When rai splutters, add green chillies. Remove from fire and pour the oil on the khandavis. Garnish with coriander.

◁ *Paalak Idlis : Recipe on page 26*

Kebab Hara Bhara

Serves 8-10 *cal/portion 65*

1 bundle (600 gm) spinach - only leaves, chopped very finely
1 cup channe ki dal (split gram), 1 tsp oil
3 slices bread - broken into pieces and churned in a mixer to get fresh crumbs
3 tbsp cornflour
2 green chillies - chopped finely
½ tsp red chilli powder, ½ tsp garam masala, ¾ tsp salt or to taste
½ tsp amchoor (dried mango powder)
½ cup grated paneer (50 gm)
¼ cup chopped green coriander

CRUSH TOGETHER
½ tsp jeera, seeds of 2 moti illaichi, 3-4 saboot kali mirch, 2-3 laung

1. Crush jeera, seeds of moti illaichi, kali mirch and laung together.
2. Clean, wash dal. Pressure cook dal with the above crushed spices, ½ tsp salt and 2 cups water. After the first whistle, keep the cooker on

slow fire for 15 minutes. Remove from fire and keep aside.
3. After the pressure drops down, mash the hot dal with a karchhi or a potato masher. If there is any water, mash the dal on fire and dry the dal as well while you are mashing it. Remove from fire.
4. Discard stems of spinach and chop leaves very finely. Wash in several changes of water. Leave the chopped spinach in the strainer for 15 minutes so that the water drains out.
5. Heat 1 tsp oil in a nonstick pan or kadhai. Squeeze and add spinach. Stir for 8-10 minutes till spinach is absolutely dry.
6. Add paneer and coriander. Cook for 1 minute. Remove from fire and keep aside.
7. Mix dal with fresh bread crumbs, cornflour, spinach-paneer, green chillies, salt and masalas. Make small balls. Flatten slightly.
8. Cook them on a tawa with just 1 tsp oil till brown on both sides. When done shift them on the sides of the tawa so that they turn crisp while more kebabs can be added in the centre of the tawa. Remove the kebabs on paper napkins.

Subz Chokker Tikki

A good way of having wheat bran, which is the fibrous portion of wheat.

Makes 10 *cal/serving 23*

1 cup (40 gm) chokker (wheat bran)
½ cup grated cauliflower, ½ cup finely chopped paalak (spinach)
1 carrot - grated, 1 potato - boiled, peeled and grated (¾ cups)
1 green chilli - chopped, 2 tbsp green coriander - chopped
¾ tsp salt, ½ tsp black pepper powder, ½ tsp chat masala
1 tsp lemon juice, seeds of 2 chhoti illaichi (green cardamom) - crushed
½ tsp honey
1-2 tbsp curd, approx., 1 tsp oil to brush the pan

1. Mix together chokker with all ingredients except oil and curd.
2. Add enough curd to chokker mixture, to bind the mixture into tikkis.
3. Heat a nonstick frying pan, brush with a little oil and brown the tikkis on both sides on medium heat. Serve hot with hari chutney.

Indian LOW FAT

Cornflakes ki Chaat

cal/serving 42 *Serves 4*

1½ cups cornflakes (Kellog's)
1 boiled potato - finely chopped, ¾ cup boiled kabuli or kaala Chanas
1 green chilli - chopped, 2 tbsp hara dhania - chopped, 1 tomato - chopped finely
½ cup curd - whisked till smooth, ¼ tsp each salt or kala namak and chilli pd.

CHUTNEY
1 tbsp amchoor, 2 tbsp sugar, ¼ cup water
½ tsp salt ½ tsp red chilli powder & ½ tsp bhuna jeera

1. For chutney, mix all ingredients. Boil. Cook for a few minutes, stirring continuously, till slightly thick. Remove from fire and keep aside.
2. Beat curd with kala namak or salt and chilli powder. Keep aside.
3. Mix potato, Chana, chilli, dhania, tomato with chutney in a big bowl.
4. Just at the time of serving, add the cornflakes. Quickly mix lightly.
5. Sprinkle some bhuna jeera (roasted cumin) powder & fresh coriander.
6. Serve immediately otherwise it tends to become soggy.

Paalak Idlis

Delicious green-paalak idlis. Tastes good even without sambhar & chutney.

Picture on page 20 *Serves 12* *cal/portion 35*

1 packet (200 gm) ready-made idli mix
1½ cups chopped spinach leaves, 2-3 green chillies - deseeded & chopped
a few blanched almonds - split into two halves, optional

TOPPING

2 cups fresh curd - beat well till smooth
½ tsp salt

TEMPERING (TADKA)

1 tbsp oil
1 tsp rai (small brown mustard seeds), ½ tsp jeera (cumin seeds)
2 green chillies - chopped
1 small tomato - chopped finely
20-30 curry leaves

Indian LOW FAT

1. Mix the idli mix according to the instructions on the packet.
2. Grind the chopped spinach and green chillies in a mixer to a smooth puree or a paste with 1-2 tbsp water.
3. Add the spinach paste to the idli mixture. Add ¼ tsp salt to it.
4. Grease a mini idli mould. Put a little batter in each cup and top with a split almond on some idlis if you wish. Steam for 14-15 minutes on medium flame till a knife inserted in the idli comes out clean. If a mini mould is not available, make small flat idlis by putting a little less batter in the normal idli mould.
5. Place the steamed idlis in a large bowl.
6. Beat the curd with salt till smooth. Pour the curd over the idlis in the bowl. Mix gently. Keep aside for 10-15 minutes.
7. Transfer the idlis to a flat serving platter or a shallow dish.
8. Heat 1 tbsp oil. Add rai and jeera. When jeera turns golden, add green chillies, tomato and curry leaves. Stir to mix all ingredients and immediately pour over the idlis covered with curd. Serve.

Curries & Wet Dishes

Indian LOW FAT

Palak Paneer

The addition of Chana masala makes this low cal vegetable very tasty.

cal/serving 97   *Serves 4-5*

600 gm (1 bunch) spinach - chopped, 2 tbsp Chana dal - cleaned and washed
4 flakes garlic, 1" piece ginger - chopped, 1 green chilli - chopped
1 onion - chopped, 5 tbsp tomato puree, 1 tsp salt, or to taste
3 tsp Chana masala, ½ tsp red chilli powder, ½ tsp sugar
75 gm paneer - cut into ½" pieces, 1 tsp ghee, 1 tsp chopped ginger

1. Pressure cook spinach with dal, onion, garlic, ginger, chilli and 1 cup water to give 1 whistle. Keep on low flame for 5 minutes.
2. Remove from fire. Cool and puree in a blender. Transfer to a kadhai.
3. Add tomato puree, salt, red chilli powder, sugar & Chana masala to the palak puree. Boil. Cook for 10 minutes on low flame.
4. Add the paneer cubes. Cook for 2-3 minutes on low flame.
5. Heat ghee. Reduce heat. Add ginger. When it turns golden, add to paalak. Serve.

Kandhari Aloo

Picture on page 48   *Serves 8*   *cal/serving 86*

Juice of red kandhari anaar (fresh red pomegranates) is added to give the curry an intriguing flavour.

½ kg baby potatoes or 5 regular potatoes
½ cup ready made tomato puree
10 almonds and 1 tbsp khus khus - soaked together in ¼ cup warm milk
1 large onion - ground to a paste
1½ tsp salt, or to taste
1 tsp degi mirch or Kashmiri laal mirch powder
1 tsp kasoori methi (dried fenugreek leaves)
2 cups anaar ke daane from 2 kandhari anaar (red pomegranates)
½ cup curd, 1 tsp cornflour or maida
1" piece ginger - cut into juliennes or match sticks, for garnishing
1 tbsp chopped coriander leaves for garnishing

Indian LOW FAT

1. Boil potatoes. Peel and keep aside. If using regular potatoes, boil small ones and cut them into 4 pieces.
2. Peel soaked almonds. Grind almonds and khus khus along with milk to a smooth paste.
3. Keeping aside 3-4 tbsp anaar ke daane (pomegranate kernels) for garnishing, take out juice of anaar by grinding the kernels (anaar ke daane) in a mixer blender without any water. Strain to get 1 cup juice.
4. In a kadhai cook onion paste for 2-3 minutes till water dries completely.
5. In a bowl, mix together - tomato puree, almond & khuskhus paste, and 1 cup water. Add this to the dried onion paste in the kadhai. Bring to a boil.
6. Add boiled potatoes, salt & chilli powder.
7. Add juice of pomegranates.
8. Add kasoori methi.
9. Reduce heat. Mix cornflour to curd and beat well to make it smooth.
10. Add curd to the potato gravy. Bring the gravy to a boil on low heat, and then simmer uncovered for 7-8 minutes. Serve hot garnished with anaar, ginger juliennes and coriander.

Kashmiri Khumb Matar

Picture on inside front cover   *Serves 6*   *cal/serving 62*

1 packet (200 gm) mushrooms (khumb)
1 cup peas (shelled) - boiled, 1 small tomato - cut into 8 pieces
½ tbsp oil plus 1 tsp oil
1½ tsp ginger-garlic paste, 1 tsp salt or to taste, ½ tsp garam masala
½ tsp degi mirch or ¼ tsp red chilli powder, ¼ tsp haldi

BOIL TOGETHER FOR 3 MINUTES AND GRIND TO A PASTE
2 onions - each cut into 4 pieces, 1 tsp saunf, ½ cup water

TOMATO PASTE (GRIND TOGETHER)
3 small tomatoes - blanched and peeled and cut into 4

2 tbsp curd, 2 laung
2-3 tbsp grated paneer (25 gm)
seeds of 2 chhoti illaichi (green cardamoms)

1. Trim stalks of mushroom and cut each into 4 pieces.

Step 1

Indian LOW FAT

2. Heat 1 tsp oil in a kadhai. Add mushrooms. Saute for 4-5 minutes on high flame till golden. Remove from fire.
3. Boil onions with saunf and water. Cook covered on low heat for 3-4 minutes. Remove from fire. Cool. Grind to a smooth paste. Keep boiled onion paste aside.
4. Boil water. Add whole tomatoes. Boil for 3-4 minutes. Remove from water. Peel and grind with all the other ingredients to a smooth paste. Keep tomato paste aside.
5. For masala, heat ½ tbsp oil. Add boiled onion paste. Cook on low heat till light golden. Add haldi.
6. Add ginger-garlic paste and tomato paste. Stir for 8-10 minutes or till dry.
7. Add degi mirch or red chilli powder.
8. Add 2 cups water. Boil. Simmer for 5 minutes.
9. Add stir fried mushrooms and boiled peas. Add salt and garam masala. Add tomato.
10. Simmer for 2 minutes till you get the right consistency. Serve.

Mixed Vegetable Curry

A delicious curry made by cooking onions in milk.

Serves 6 *cal/serving 57*

½ cup milk
1 onion - ground to a paste, 1 tsp ginger-garlic paste
1 tbsp oil
1½ tsp salt, or to taste, ½ tsp haldi
½ tsp red chilli powder, 1 tsp garam masala, 1½ tsp jeera powder
2 tbsp chopped green coriander, 1 tbsp kasoori methi

GRIND TOGETHER
½ cup curd, 2 tsp cornflour
2 tomatoes - chopped

VEGETABLES (3 CUPS CHOPPED)
8 medium florets of cauliflower (¼ of a cauliflower)
2 small carrots - cut into small pieces (¼" pieces), about 1 cup chopped
10 french beans - chopped, ½ cup shelled peas

Indian LOW FAT

1. Cut all vegetables and wash them.
2. All the vegetables are cut into small pieces, except the cauliflower which is cut into medium size florets.
3. In a kadhai put onion, garlic-ginger and ½ cup milk. Cook for 3-4 minutes till milk dries.
4. Add the vegetables to the onion mixture. Add 1 tbsp oil. Mix well for 2-3 minutes on low heat.
5. Add tomato paste, salt, haldi, red chilli powder, jeera powder, garam masala and coriander. Cook, stirring on medium heat for 4-5 minutes or till the curd gets well blended and turns dry.
6. Add 2 cups water and kasoori methi. Cook for about 8-10 minutes on low heat without covering, till the vegetables are crisp-tender and a thick gravy remains. Serve hot.

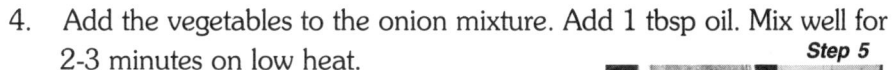

Saunfiyaan Dhania Paneer

Picture on page 38 *Serves 4* *cal/serving 106*

200 gms paneer - cut into ½" square pieces
1 tbsp oil
1 onion - finely chopped
1" piece ginger & 8-10 flakes garlic - crushed to a paste or 2 tsp ginger-garlic paste
½ tsp red chilli powder, ½ tsp garam masala
1 tsp salt, or to taste, 1 tsp dhania powder
1 cup milk
2 tbsp chopped coriander

CORIANDER PASTE

¾ cup chopped coriander
2 green chillies
1 tbsp saunf (fennel)
½ cup milk

Cabbage Pea Poriyal : Recipe on page 60 ➢

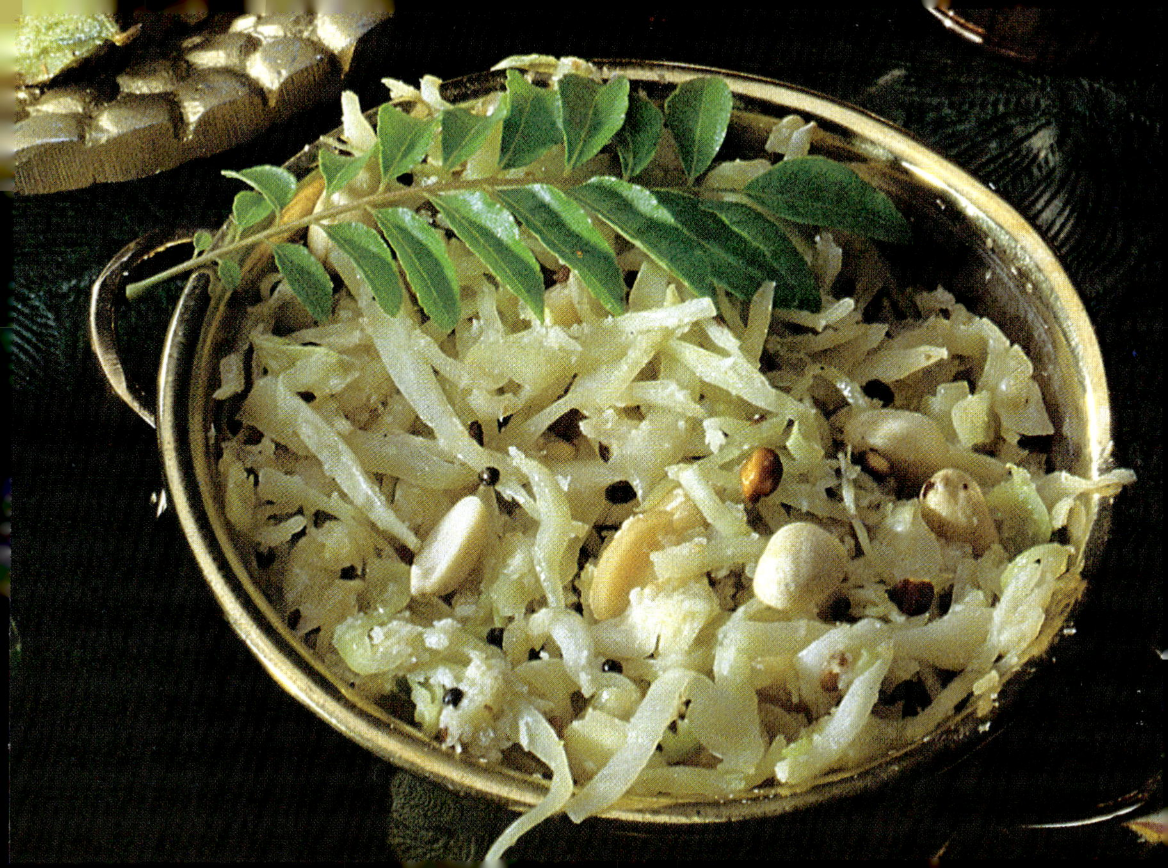

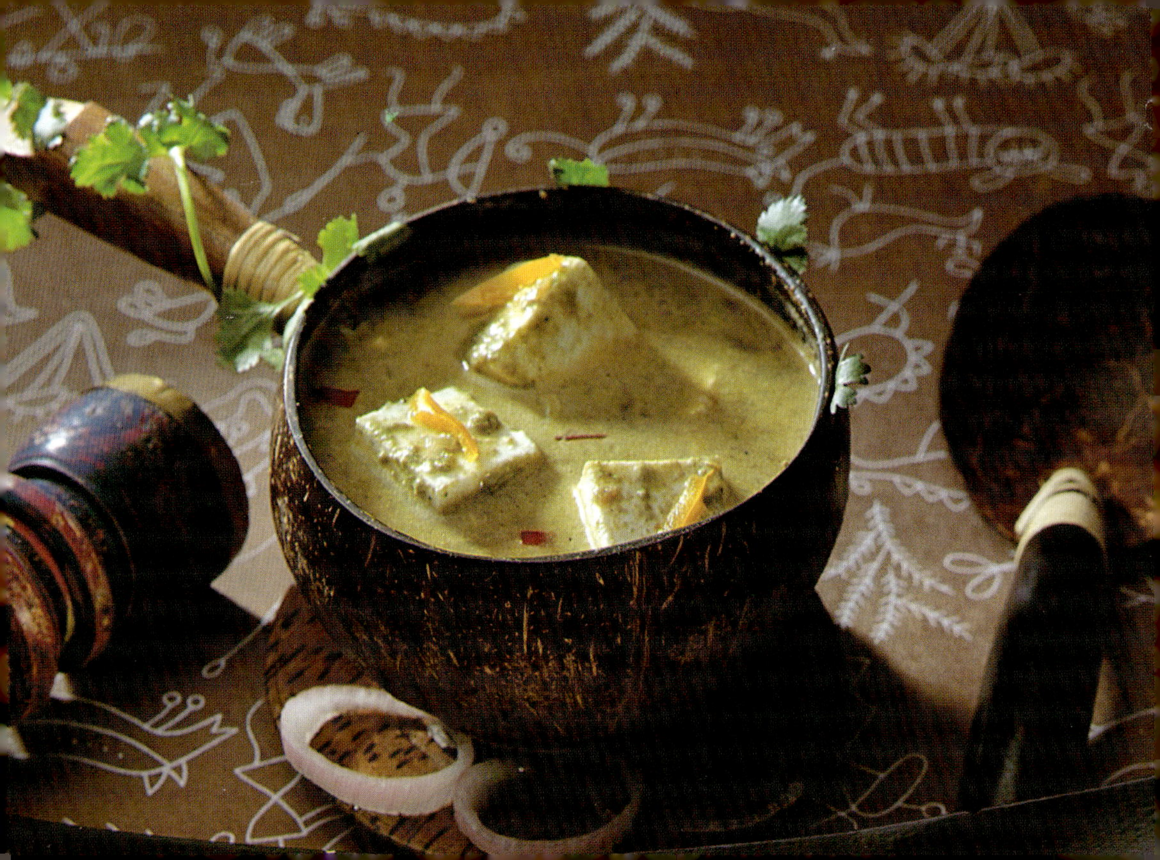

Indian LOW FAT

1. Mix all the ingredients given under coriander paste to a thin paste in a mixer.
2. Heat 1 tbsp oil in a kadhai and add the chopped onions. Fry till golden.
3. Add the ginger-garlic paste, stir for few seconds.
4. Reduce heat, add the prepared coriander paste. Cook for 2 minutes.
5. On medium flame, add red chilli powder, garam masala and dhania powder. Mix well. Keep scraping sides if masala sticks to the sides/bottom of the kadhai. Stir till masala turns dry.
6. Add ½ cup of water. Boil, stirring at intervals. Remove from fire. Let the gravy cool down a little.
7. Add milk, mix well. Add paneer and return to fire and cook stirring continuously on low heat for 3-4 minutes.
8. Serve hot, garnished with chopped coriander.

◁ *Saunfiyan Dhania Paneer : Recipe on page 36*

Baked Kofta Curry

cal/serving 40   *Serves 4*

100 gm lauki (bottle gourd) - grated (1 cup)
1 boiled potato - mashed
2 tbsp besan (gram flour) - roasted
1 tbsp chopped coriander, 1 green chilli - chopped
½ tsp salt, or to taste, ¼ tsp haldi
½ tsp each of red chilli powder, garam masala, amchoor

GRAVY
1 tsp oil
1 tsp jeera (cumin seeds)
1½ tsp ginger paste
1 cup ready made tomato puree
2 tsp dhania powder, 1 tsp salt, or to taste
¼ tsp haldi, ¼ tsp red chilli powder
½ tsp garam masala

Indian LOW FAT

1. Grate the bottle gourd finely. Dry roast the besan for 2 minutes in a heavy bottomed kadhai on low flame.
2. Mix lauki, besan, mashed potato, green chilli, coriander, salt, red chilli powder, amchoor, haldi and garam masala. Mix well.
3. Make small balls out of the mixture with oiled hands.
4. Cover an oven tray with aluminium foil. Grease it lightly. Place koftas on it. Keep the balls or koftas in a hot oven at 200°C for 20-25 minutes till done. Keep aside.
5. To prepare the gravy, heat 1 tsp oil in a non stick kadhai. Add jeera.
6. After it turns golden, add ginger paste. Mix well.
7. Add tomato puree and all the masalas given under the gravy. Reduce flame and stir for 3-4 minutes till puree turns dry. Add 2 cups water. Boil. Simmer on low heat for 4-5 minutes.
8. Add the baked balls or koftas. Simmer for a minute. Sprinkle with fresh coriander leaves and serve hot.

Step 3

Step 7

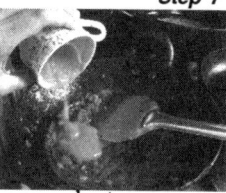

Chana & Nugget Curry

An unusual curry in which the onions are steamed to make the gravy.

Serves 4   *cal/serving 77*

½ cup kabuli Chanas (chick peas) - soaked for 5-6 hours or overnight
2 moti illaichi (black cardamoms), 1" stick dalchini (cinnamon)
½ cup soya chunks (10-12 pieces) - soaked in water
1 tsp oil
2 tomatoes - ground to a puree
1 tsp dhania powder (ground coriander)
½ tsp garam masala and ¼ tsp red chilli powder
¼ tsp each of amchoor and haldi, 1 tsp salt
2-3 tbsp chopped green coriander

GRIND TOGETHER
2 onions,
1" piece ginger, 1 green chilli
1 tsp jeera

Indian LOW FAT

1. Soak soya chunks in hot water for 15-20 minutes. Keep aside.
2. Drain water from Chanas. Add 3 cups water, moti illaichi and dalchini. Pressure cook to give 1 whistle and then keep on low heat for 8 minutes. Remove from fire and keep aside.
3. Grind onions, ginger, green chilli and cumin seeds to a paste with ¼ cup water. Put in a pressure cooker without any oil and pressure cook to give 2 whistles. Remove from fire.
4. When the pressure drops, add 1 tsp oil.
5. Squeeze soya chunks and add to the onion masala. Bhuno on medium heat for 3-4 minutes.
6. Reduce heat. Add all masalas - dhania powder, garam masala, red chilli powder, amchoor, haldi and salt. Stir for 2 minutes on low flame.
7. Add the fresh tomato puree. Cook for 4-5 minutes, till dry.
8. Add Chanas along with water and chopped coriander. Keep on low flame for 2-3 minutes. Serve hot.

Step 1

Paneer Makhani

A makhani dish without butter and yet you do not miss the butter!

Serves 4-5 *cal/serving 100*

250 gm paneer - cut into 1" cubes
1 cup readymade tomato puree
1 tbsp oil, ½ tsp jeera (cumin seeds)
4-5 flakes garlic and 1" piece ginger - ground to a paste (1½ tsp ginger-garlic paste)
1 tbsp kasoori methi (dry fenugreek leaves)
1 tsp tomato ketchup
2 tsp dhania powder, ½ tsp garam masala
1 tsp salt, or to taste, ½ tsp red chilli powder, preferably degi mirch
½ cup water
½-1 cup milk, approx.

GARNISH
1 green chilli - cut into thin long pieces, fresh coriander

Indian LOW FAT

1. Heat oil in a kadhai. Reduce heat. Add jeera. When it turns golden, add ginger-garlic paste.
2. When paste starts to change colour add tomato puree & cook till dry.
3. Add kasoori methi and tomato ketchup.
4. Add masalas - dhania powder, garam masala, salt and red chilli powder. Mix well for a few seconds. Cook till dry.
5. Add ½ cup water. Boil. Simmer on low heat for 4-5 minutes. Reduce heat.
6. Add the paneer cubes. Remove from fire. Keep aside to cool for atleast 5-10 minutes, or preferably longer.
7. Add enough milk to the cold paneer masala to get a thick curry, mix gently. (Remember to add milk only after the masala is no longer hot, to prevent the milk from curdling. After adding milk, heat curry on low heat.)
8. Keep on low heat, stirring continuously till just about to boil.
9. Remove from fire immediately and transfer to a serving dish. Serve garnished with long, thin pieces of green chilli and coriander.

Water Melon Curry

An unusual & spicy, thin reddish curry. Water melon is all water, so the curry is really low fat.

Serves 4 *cal/serving 46*

4 cups of tarbooz (water melon) - cut into 1" pieces along with a little white portion also, and deseeded
4-5 flakes garlic - crushed
½ tbsp oil, ½ tsp jeera (cumin seeds)
a pinch of hing (asafoetida)
1 tbsp ginger - cut into thin match sticks (jullienes)
½ tsp dhania (coriander) powder
½ - ¾ tsp chilli powder, a pinch of haldi powder, ½ tsp salt, or to taste
2 tsp lemon juice

GARNISH
sliced green chillies & chopped green coriander

Moong Stuffed Tinda : Recipe on page 70 ➢

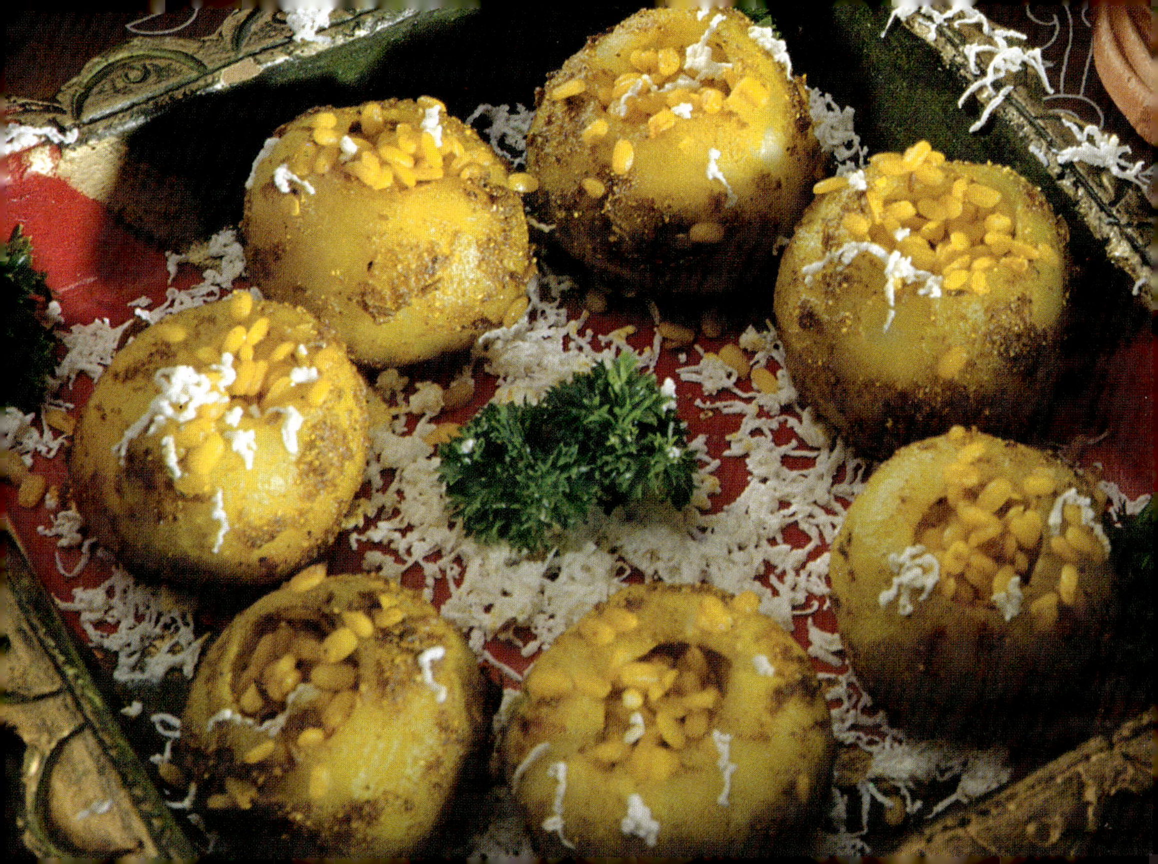

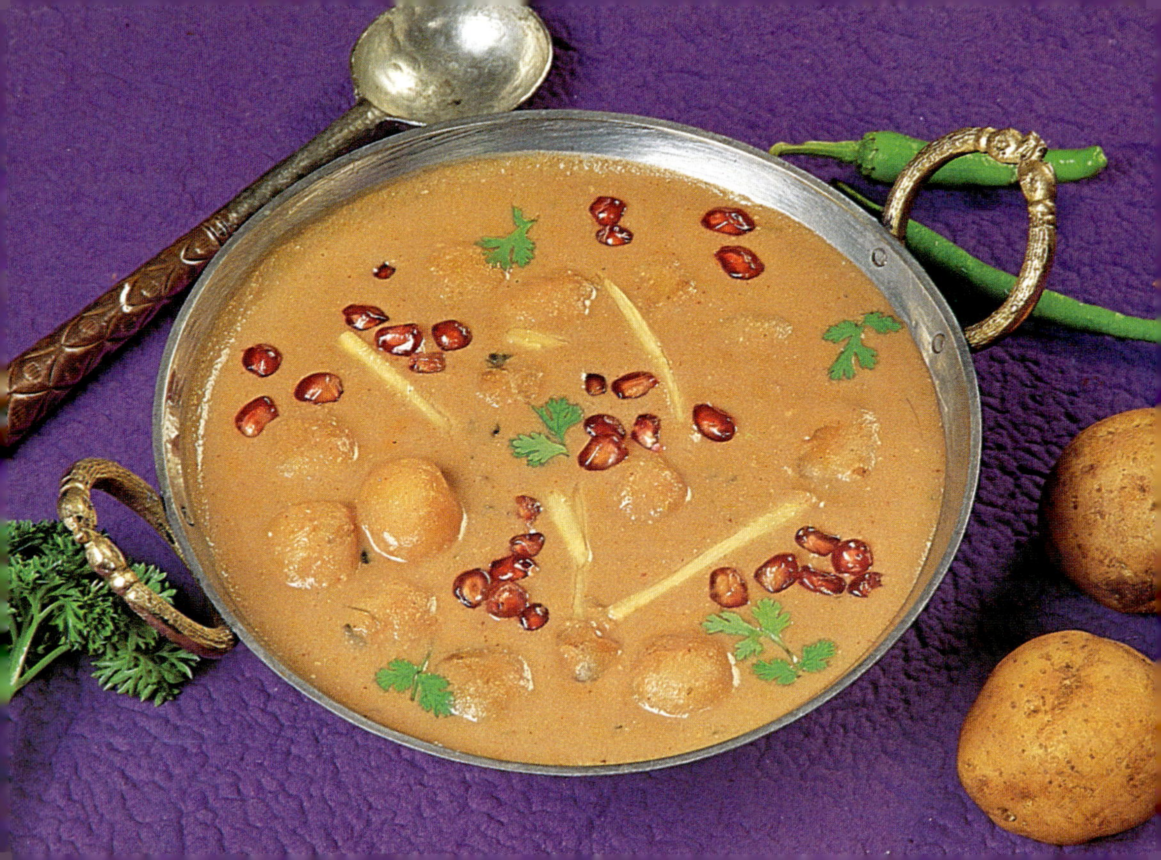

Indian LOW FAT

1. Puree 1½ cups of water-melon cubes (the upper soft pieces) with 4-5 flakes of garlic in a mixer to get 1 cup of water melon puree. Leave the remaining firm, lower pieces (with the white portion) as it is. Keep aside.
2. Heat oil in a kadhai. Add hing and jeera. Let jeera turn golden.
3. Add garlic & shredded ginger & stir for ½ minute.
4. Add the remaining water melon pieces or cubes and stir to mix.
5. Sprinkle coriander powder, red chilli powder and haldi. Stir for ½ minute.
6. Add the water melon puree, salt and lemon juice. Simmer for 2-3 minutes till you get a thin curry. Remove from fire.
7. Garnish with green chillies and green coriander. Serve hot.

Step 2

◁ *Kandhari Aloo: Recipe on page 30*

Dal Makhani (without makhan)

Picture on page 2   *Serves 6*   *cal/serving 75*

1 cup kaali dal (saboot urad)
1 large onion - ground to a paste, 6-8 flakes garlic - crushed (1 tsp paste)
1½ tsp salt, or to taste, ¼ tsp red chilli powder
½ cup tomato puree, 1 tsp jeera powder, ½ tsp garam masala
1 tsp kasoori methi, 1 cup milk approx, some whipped curd to garnish

1. Soak the kaali dal overnight. Drain water and wash several times.
2. Pressure cook kaali dal with one ground onion, crushed garlic, salt, red chilli powder and enough water (about 5 cups) to give 1 whistle and keep on low flame for 20 minutes. Remove from fire. Let it cool.
3. Add tomato puree, jeera powder, garam masala & kasoori methi. Boil. Keep on low flame for 20 minutes. Remove from fire. Keep aside.
4. At serving time, add 1 cup milk to get the right consistency. Cook for 4-5 minutes on low heat to get the right colour and consistency. Garnish with coriander and a swirl of whipped curd, using a spoon. Serve.

Dry & Semidry Dishes

Make balls of a potato with the help of a melon scooper

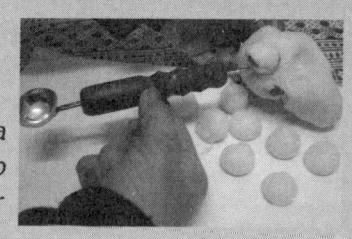

Mili Juli Subzi

Picture on cover *Serves 6-8* *cal/serving 70*

1 large potato - peeled, scooped to form small balls (about 8 balls)
200 gm (1 packet) baby cabbage or brussel sprouts (15-20 pieces) - trim the stalk end or ½ of a small cabbage - cut into 1" pieces
100 gms baby corns (7-8) - keep whole if small or cut into 2 pieces if big
¼ cup peas (matar), 6-7 French beans - cut into ¼" pieces (½ cup)
1 carrot - cut into ¼" pieces (½ cup)
12-15 baby onions or 3 regular onions of small size - cut into 4
15 cherry tomatoes or 2 regular small tomatoes - cut into 4, remove pulp
¼ tsp haldi, 1 tsp salt, ½ tsp red chilli powder, ½ tsp garam masala
½ tsp degi mirch, 1½ tbsp oil

BOILED ONION PASTE

1 onion, 2 laung, seeds of 2 chhoti illaichi (green cardamoms), ½ cup water

TOMATO PASTE

2 tbsp curd, 2 tbsp grated paneer
2 tomatoes - put in boiling hot water for 3-4 minutes and peeled (blanched)

Indian LOW FAT

1. Make balls of a potato with the help of a melon scooper (see page 51).
2. Boil 7 cups water with 2 tsp salt. Add potato balls. Boil for 3 minutes. Add cabbage, baby corns, peas, beans and carrots. Boil for a minute. Remove from fire. Strain, put in cold water and strain again.
3. Heat 1 tbsp oil. Add whole onions. Saute for 2 minutes till soft. Add cherry tomatoes or big pieces of tomato. Stir.
4. Add all the boiled vegetables. Sprinkle ½ tsp salt. Saute for 1 minute. Remove from fire. Keep aside.
5. For onion paste, boil onions with all the ingredients of onion paste for 3-4 minutes on low heat. Cool and grind to a paste. Keep aside.
6. Grind all the ingredients of tomato paste to a paste. Keep aside.
7. For masala, heat ½ tbsp oil, add onion paste. Stir for a minute on low heat. Add haldi. Mix well.
8. Add tomato paste. Stir for 8-10 minutes till dry.
9. Add salt and red chilli powder. Add ¾ cup water, ½ tsp garam masala and degi mirch. Boil. Cook for ½ a minute.
10. Add stir fried vegetables. Mix well for 2-3 minutes. Serve hot garnished with a blanched floret of broccoli.

Sambhari Bhindi

Picture on page 58 *Serves 4-5* *cal/serving 42*

250 gm bhindi (lady fingers), 1 large onion - cut into 8 pieces
2 tbsp finely chopped coriander, 2 whole green chillies
3 tbsp curd, 1 tomato - cut into four, pulp removed and chopped

FILLING
1¼ tsp salt, 3 tbsp sambhar powder, 2 tsp saunf (fennel)

1. Wash, dry bhindi. Cut a thin slice from the cap end of each bhindi. Make a slit lengthwise for filling. Peel onion, cut each into 8 pieces.
2. Mix salt, sambhar powder and saunf. Stuff the masala in the bhindi.
3. Place bhindi and onions in a shallow borosil dish. Sprinkle the leftover masala if any, over the onions. Mix well. Cover with an aluminium foil and cook in an oven for 20 minutes at 180°C. Remove from oven.
4. To the cooked bhindi in the bowl, add beaten curd, coriander, green chillies and tomato pieces. Mix well and keep aside till serving time.
5. At serving time, heat in the oven without covering for 7-8 minutes.

Indian LOW FAT

Nugget Keema

Serves 4-6 *cal/serving 81*

1½ cups nutri nugget granules (keema)-soaked in 2 cups warm water for ½ hour
1 cup boiled peas, 1½ cups curd, ¼ tsp red chilli powder, 1¼ tsp salt
2 tbsp finely chopped green coriander, 10-12 flakes of garlic - crushed to a paste
1" piece ginger - finely chopped, 2 tbsp tomato puree

DRY ROAST ON A TAWA AND GRIND COARSELY
5-6 saboot kalimirch, 4-5 laung (cloves), seeds of 2 moti illaichi, 1 tsp jeera

1. Wash the soaked granules several times. Drain and squeeze the water.
2. Mix curd, 1¼ tsp salt, ¼ tsp chilli powder, chopped dhania & garlic.
3. Soak the nuggets in the curd for at least ½ hour so that the granules absorb the spice flavour well.
4. In a kadhai put the marinated granules. Keep on fire. Add roasted and ground spices. Cook till almost dry.
5. Add boiled peas, chopped ginger and tomato puree. Stir for 3-4 minutes till dry. Do not dry too much. Serve hot.

Khatti Mithi Subzi

Picture on page 86 *Serves 6* *cal/serving 75*

1 tsp oil
1 large onion - chopped
3 thin carrots - cut into 1¼" long, thin fingers (about 2½ cups)
1 capsicum - cut into ½" pieces
1 cup peas - boiled
3-4 flakes garlic - crushed
½" piece ginger - finely chopped (1 tsp)
4 tomatoes - roasted, peeled and chopped
1½ tsp salt, or to taste
1 tbsp tomato puree
1 tbsp vinegar
½ tsp black pepper powder
1 tsp sugar
2 tsp cornflour dissolved in ½ cup water

Tandoori Paneer ki Subzi : Recipe on page 88 ➢

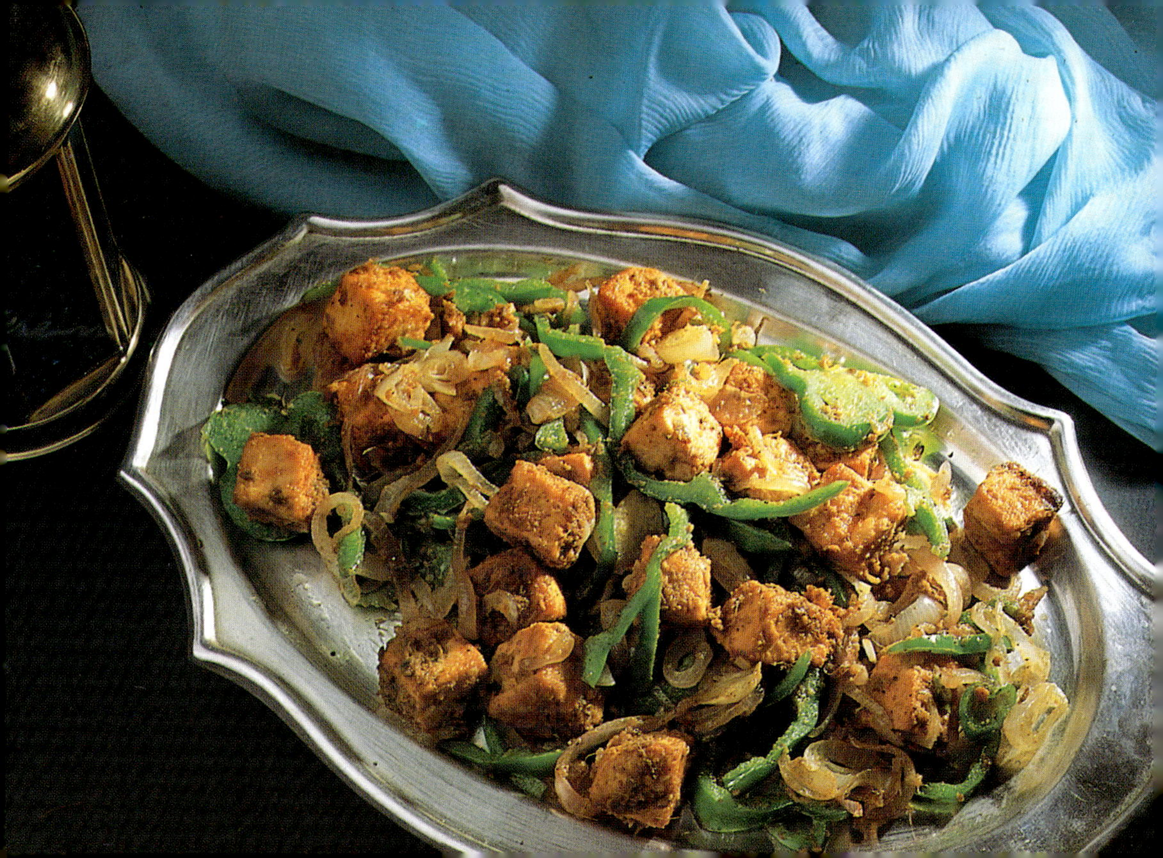

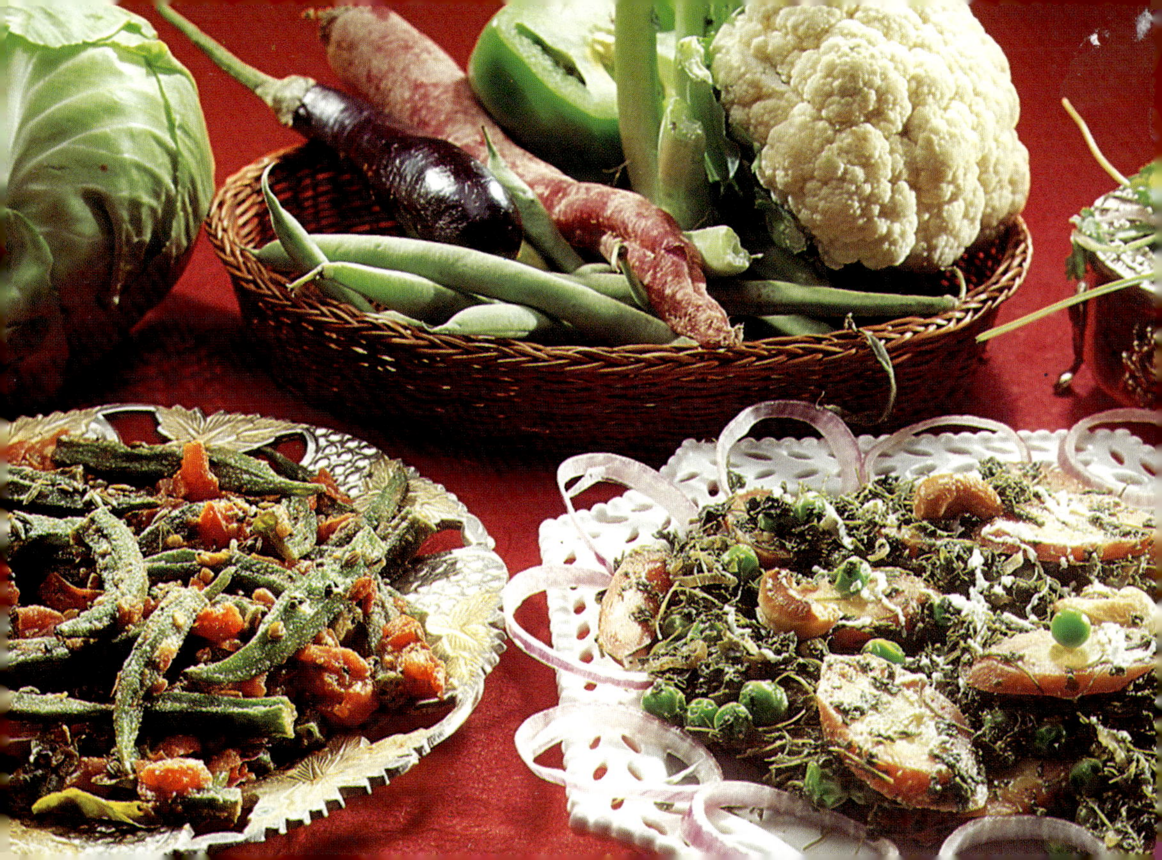

Indian LOW FAT

1. Pierce a washed tomato on a fork deeply and hold it over a naked flame for 2-3 minutes to blacken and loosen the skin. Peel. Do not wash. Chop the roasted tomatoes.
2. In a kadhai, put 1 tsp oil. Add chopped onions, ginger and garlic. Stir on low heat for 1 minute.
3. Add carrots. Stir for 1 minute. Add ½ cup water and salt. Cook for 2-3 minutes without covering.
4. Add the chopped tomatoes. Cook for 4-5 minutes on medium heat till carrots get done and are crunchy. Do not cover and do not over cook.
5. Add tomato puree, vinegar, black pepper powder and 1 tsp of sugar. Mix well together.
6. Add the boiled peas and capsicum. Mix well.
7. Add cornflour paste and stir for 2-3 minutes till sauce turns thick. Serve hot.

◁ *Sambhari Bhindi : Recipe on page 54*
◁ *Kastoori Gajar Matar : Recipe on page 76*

Cabbage Pea Poriyal

A dry, spicy South Indian side dish.

Picture on page 37 *Serves 4-5* *cal/serving 90*

½ kg cabbage (1 medium) - chopped finely, ½ cup shelled peas
1 tsp roasted peanuts, optional
1½ tsp salt, or to taste

TEMPERING (CHOWNK)
1 tbsp oil
1 tsp rai (mustard seeds), ½ tsp jeera (cumin seeds)
2 tsp urad dal (split black gram), 2 tsp Chana dal (bengal gram dal)
2 red chillies - broken into bits and deseeded
½ tsp hing (asafoetida), ¼ cup curry leaves

PASTE (GRIND TOGETHER)
2 green chillies - deseeded and chopped
4-5 tbsp grated coconut - remove the brown skin and then grate
1 onion - chopped, 1 tsp jeera, 2 tbsp curd

Indian LOW FAT

1. Heat 1 tbsp oil. Reduce heat. Collect all ingredients of tempering together. Add to the oil. Stir for a minute on low heat.
2. When dals turn golden, add the chopped cabbage.
3. Add salt and 2 tbsp water.
4. Add peas. Cover & cook on low heat for 7-8 minutes till peas turn tender.
5. Add the coconut paste. Stir fry for 3-4 minutes. Serve hot garnished with roasted peanuts.

Step 1

Note: You can make any poriyal in the same way - carrot, beetroot or capsicum.

Saunfiyan Tori Tukri

Stuffed tori with the fragrant flavour of fennel. A green vegetable made delicious!

Picture on backcover   Serves 4   cal/serving 47

250 gm (4) tori (zuchhini) - peel thinly & cut each into 2" pieces to get 2-3" long pieces and make a silt lengthwise in each piece
1 tbsp oil

DRY MASALAS

½ tsp haldi, 1½ tsp dhania (coriander) powder
¼ tsp garam masala, ¼-½ tsp red chilli powder
½ tsp amchoor, ¾ tsp salt

FILLING (GRIND TOGETHER TO A PASTE WITHOUT WATER)

1 large onion - chopped
3-4 flakes garlic, ½" piece ginger
1½ tsp saunf (fennel)

Indian LOW FAT

1. Grind together all the ingredients of the filling in a grinder without water. Grind to a fine paste.
2. Add haldi, dhania powder, garam masala and red chilli powder to the prepared paste. Mix well.
3. Peel tori thinly and cut each into 2" pieces to get 2-3 long pieces from each tori. Make a silt in each piece lengthwise, for the filling.
4. Fill or stuff the tori nicely with the prepared filling. Pat the remaining paste on top of the toris.
5. Heat 1 tbsp oil in kadhai. Stir fry the stuffed tori in hot oil. Stir gently to mix.
6. Cover with a wet lid and cook for 8-10 minutes or till done. Stir once in between. Remove from fire and serve hot.

Hara Pyaz Khumb

Mushrooms with spring onions. This vegetable tastes best if served fresh from the stove because the spring onions loose their crispness on keeping.

Serves 4   *cal/serving 88*

200 gms (1 packet) fresh mushrooms
½ cup fresh curd of skimmed milk - beaten well with a spoon
5-6 spring onions - diagonally cut into small pieces, up to ¾ of it's green leaves
1 green chilli - deseeded & chopped
2 tsp oil
6-8 flakes garlic - crushed
2 tsp dhania (coriander) powder
a pinch of sugar
¼ tsp red chilli powder
1 tsp salt
2 laung (cloves) - crushed roughly

Indian LOW FAT

1. Wash mushrooms. Cut mushrooms into half if they are small and into 4 pieces, if they are big.
2. Heat 2 tsp oil in kadhai/pan. Add mushrooms and stir fry for 3-4 minutes on medium flame, till they turn soft and light brown.
3. Add garlic. Saute for 1 minute on low flame.
4. Keeping the heat low, add beaten curd. Stir fry for 3-4 minutes on low flame, till it dries.
5. Add crushed laung. Cook for ½ minute.
6. Add coriander powder, salt, red chilli powder and sugar to it. Cook for 1-2 minutes. Keep aside till serving time.
7. At serving time, add green onions and chopped green chillies. Cook for 3-4 minutes on low flame. Remove from fire and serve hot.

Note: If spring onions are not available, use 1 capsicum and 2 small, ordinary onions, cut into thin slices.

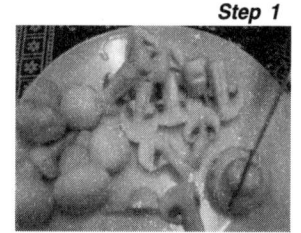

Safed Jalpari

The water vegetable - lotus stem is coated with a white yogurt paste and stir fried to a delicious dry dish.

Picture on facing page　　　*Serves 5-6*　　　*cal/serving 146*

300 gm (2 medium) bhein or kamal kakri (lotus stem) - cut into diagonal thick pieces
3 onions - each cut into 4 pieces and separated
2 tbsp oil, 1 tsp ajwain (carom seeds)
¼ tsp haldi, ¼ tsp salt, ¼ tsp red chilli powder
2-3 tbsp chopped coriander

MARINADE
1½ cups curd - hang for ½ hour
1 tsp ajwain (carom seeds)
1 tbsp finely chopped coriander
1½ tbsp besan (gram flour)
1 tbsp ginger garlic paste, 1 tbsp oil

Contd...

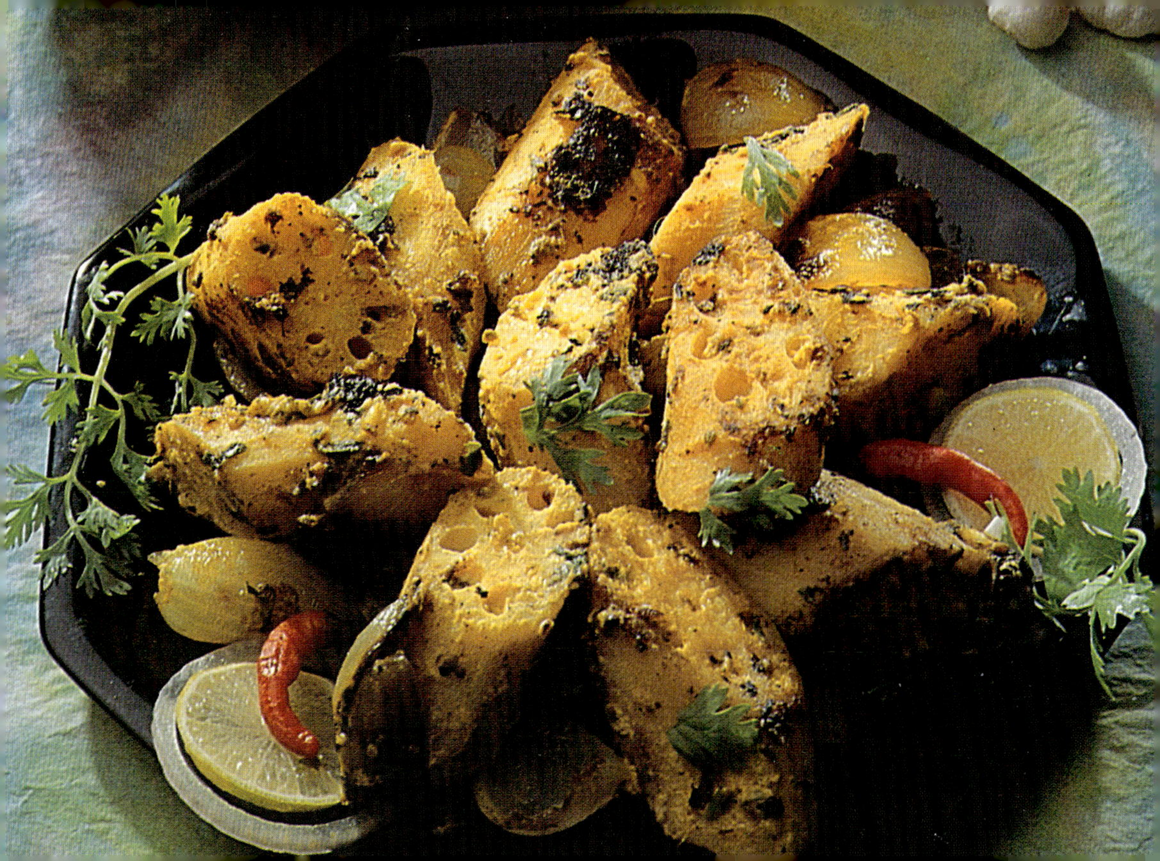

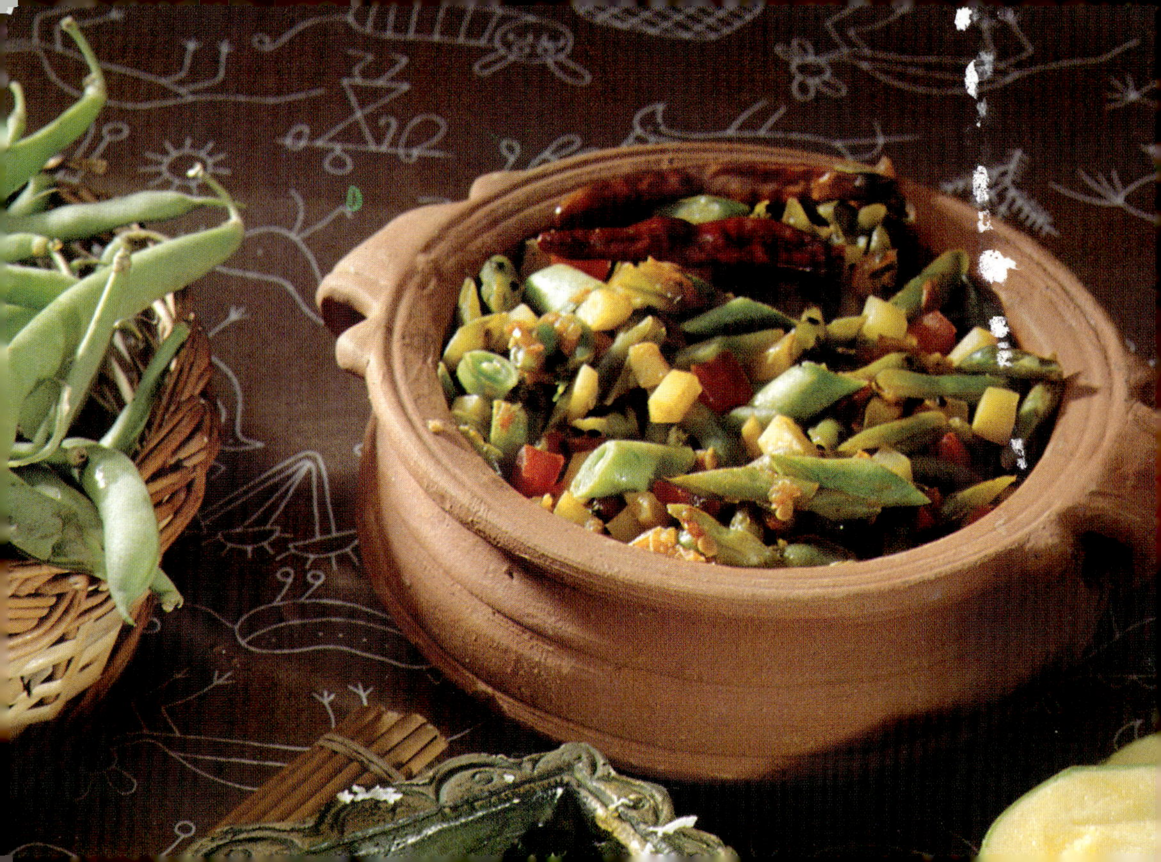

— Indian LOW FAT

1 tsp salt, ½ tsp red chilli powder, ½ tsp haldi
1½ tsp dhania powder
½ tsp garam masala

TO SERVE
some chaat masala

1. Peel bhein. Cut into diagonal pieces of 1" thickness.
2. Put bhein in a pan with 3-4 cups water and 1 tsp salt. Keep on fire. Boil. Reduce heat and cook covered for about 8 minutes on low heat. Remove from fire.
3. Mix all ingredients of the marinade together.
4. Add the boiled pieces of bhein to the marinade. Mix well to coat nicely.
5. Heat 2 tbsp oil in a kadhai. Add ajwain and wait till golden.
6. Add onions. Stir till golden.
7. Add haldi, salt and red chilli powder. Mix.
8. Add the marinated bhein along with all the marinade. Cook on low heat, keeping the vegetable spread out. Cook covered till bhein turns golden. Add coriander. Mix well. Serve sprinkled with chaat masala.

◁ *Phalli Tamatar Kairi : Recipe on page 82*

Moong Stuffed Tinda

Picture on page 47   *Serves 4*   *cal/serving* 139

500 gm (8-10) tinda (round gourd) - firm, medium sized
½ tsp salt, juice of 1 lemon, 2 tsp ginger paste
2 tsp dhania powder, ½ tsp garam masala, ¼ tsp red chilli powder, ½ tsp haldi
a few tooth picks

FILLING

75 gm (½ cup) dhuli moong dal - soaked for 2 hours
½ cup (50 gm) grated paneer, 1 tbsp oil
a pinch of hing (asafoetida), ½ tsp jeera (cumin seeds)
1 green chilli - finely chopped, ½" piece ginger - finely chopped
½ tsp dhania powder, ½ tsp red chilli powder, ¼ tsp haldi, ¾ tsp salt - to taste

1. Wash tindas. Scrape tindas and cut a thin slice from the top. Keep the thin slice (cap) aside. Scoop out tindas to make them hollow. Do not scoop to much.
2. Mix salt, lemon juice & ginger-paste. Rub this inside-outside of tindas.
3. Drain the soaked dal in a strainer.

Indian LOW FAT

4. Heat 1 tbsp oil in a heavy bottomed kadhai. Add a pinch of hing. Wait for 5-10 seconds. Add jeera. Let jeera turn golden brown.
5. Reduce flame. Add ginger and green chilli. Mix.
6. Add dhania powder, red chilli powder and haldi.
7. Add dal. Add salt to taste and cook covered on low flame for about 8-10 minutes or till dal is done. Sprinkle a little water in-between, if it sticks to the bottom of the kadhai.
8. Add paneer and mix well. Remove from fire.
9. Stuff the dal filling inside the scooped out tindas. Press well. Cover with the cap. Secure the cap with a toothpick.
10. Heat 1 tbsp oil in a kadhai. Add ½ tsp jeera and fry till golden.
11. Reduce flame and add 2 tsp dhania powder, ½ tsp garam masala, ¼ tsp red chilli powder and ½ tsp haldi.
12. Add the stuffed tindas one by one. Gently turn them lightly, to coat the oil all over. Cover & cook on low flame for 15-20 minutes till they feel soft when a knife is inserted in them. Keep turning sides in-between to brown the tindas evenly. Sprinkle some water in-between if required.
13. To serve, remove caps and grate some paneer finely on the hot tindas.

Saunf-Imli waale Baingan

Brinjals have a very low calorie content of their own so if made oil free, they are really light in calories.

Serves 3-4 cal/serving 20

250 gm small baingan (brinjals)
2 tsp imli (tamarind) pulp (pulp of a small marble sized ball of tamarind)
1 tsp sugar

DRY MASALAS
1 tsp salt, ½ tsp red chilli, ½ tsp haldi, 1 tsp amchoor, ½ tsp garam masala

DRY ROAST LIGHTLY AND POWDER
1 tbsp saunf (aniseeds)
2 tsp saboot dhania (coriander seeds)

GARNISH
1 onion - cut into rings
1 green chilli - cut lengthwise thinly

Indian LOW FAT

1. Wash the baingan and give 2 crosswise cuts to slit into four with the base intact.
2. Mix all the dry masalas. Add the roasted and ground saunf and dhania too. Mix 2 tsp of water with the masala to make it wet.
3. Fill the masala in the baingans properly.
4. In a non stick pan, add half cup water and the brinjals. Cook covered on low flame for 15-20 minutes till they turn soft, turning gently, occasionally to cook the brinjals well from all sides. Cook till the water dries and the brinjals turn very soft.
5. Mix imli pulp with a little water and sugar. Add imli to the cooked brinjals. Stir for 2-3 minutes on fire.
6. Serve hot, garnished with green chillies and onion rings.

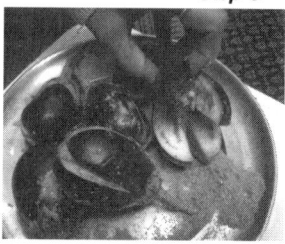

Step 3

Pao Bhaji Masala Gobi

Cauliflower flavoured with pao bhaji masala and toasted sesame seeds.

Serves 4 *cal/serving 75*

MIX TOGETHER IN A BOWL

1 medium size, about 400 gm cauliflower (phool gobi) - cut into medium florets
½ cup thick fresh curd
1 tsp garlic paste (6-7 flakes garlic), 1 tsp ginger paste (1" piece ginger)
1 tsp salt, or to taste, ½ tsp haldi
1 tsp pao bhaji masala, or to taste

OTHER INGREDIENTS

3 tsp oil
1 tsp til (sesame seeds) - dry roasted on a tawa, ½ tsp pao bhaji masala
1 potato - boiled, peeled & cut into 1" pieces
3-4 tbsp finely chopped coriander leaves (hara dhania)
½ tomato - finely chopped

Indian LOW FAT

1. Cut gobi into medium florets. Wah and wipe dry.
2. Mix curd, garlic, ginger, salt, haldi and pao bhaji masala in a big bowl.
3. Add the gobi florets. Mix well to coat all the florets. Keep aside.
4. Heat 1 tsp oil in a kadhai. Add a pinch of haldi. Add the boiled aloos. Sprinkle ¼ tsp salt and ½ tsp pao bhaji masala. Stir fry for a few minutes till they turn brownish. Add the chopped coriander and mix well to coat the aloos. Remove from kadhai.
5. Heat 2 more tsp oil in a kadhai. Add the gobi along with the curd. Stir for 1-2 minutes. Cover and reduce heat. Cook covered on low flame, for about 10 minutes, till the gobhi is done.
6. Uncover and stir on medium flame for 2-3 minutes and dry the curd.
7. Add the tomato and potatoes. Mix well for a minute.
8. Transfer to a serving dish. Sprinkle some pao bhaji masala and roasted til. Serve hot.

Kastoori Gajar Matar

Dry fenugreek is mixed with carrots and some green peas to make a very colourful dish. Milk is added to dry fenugreek leaves to freshen them.

Picture on page 58   Serves 4-5   cal/serving 129

3 carrots - peeled, cut into half lengthwise & sliced diagonally or cut into ¼" cubes
1 packet (2 cups) kasoori methi (dried fenugreek leaves) - cleaned & soaked in water for ½ hour
1½ cups shelled peas (matar) - boiled
1 large onion - chopped
1 cup milk
2 tbsp mustard oil or any refined oil
a pinch of sugar
1 tsp salt, a pinch of amchoor (dried mango powder)
½ tsp red chilli powder, ½ tsp garam masala

Indian LOW FAT

1. Soak cleaned methi in water for at least ½ hour or even more. Strain.
2. Squeeze very well. Chop finely and keep aside. Peel and cut carrots into half lengthwise & slice diagonally.
3. Heat 2 tbsp oil in a clean kadhai. Add onion and cook till soft.
4. Add kasoori methi and milk.
5. Add carrots. Cook on low heat till carrots are done and the milk is almost dry.
6. Add a pinch of sugar. Mix well.
7. Add salt and red chilli powder. Cook for 1 minute.
8. Add peas. Add garam masala and amchoor. Uncover and stir fry for 2-3 minutes. Serve hot.

Step 1

Step 2

Bread Dahi Badas

Prepare at least 1 hour before serving, for the bread to soak the dahi.

Serves 4-5 *cal/serving 96*

4 slices of fresh bread, preferably whole wheat bread
2 cups thick curd (of toned milk) - beat till smooth
¾ tsp bhuna jeera powder
½ tsp red chilli powder
¼ tsp kala namak, 1 tsp salt, or to taste

OTHER INGREDIENTS
1 tbsp finely chopped fresh coriander
some hari chutney, optional

MITHI CHUTNEY
1 tbsp amchoor (dry mango powder)
2 tbsp sugar, salt to taste
¼ tsp red chilli powder, ¼ tsp garam masala, ¼ tsp bhuna jeera powder

Indian LOW FAT

1. Whip curd. Mix salt and all the other spices to get a raita.
2. Cut sides of bread and arrange 2 slices in a shallow rectangular dish.
3. Spread 2-3 tbsp of raita on each piece of bread. Cover both slices with the other 2 slices of bread.
4. Pour the left over dahi on them to cover completely. Let the dahi cover the empty spaces of the dish also.
5. Sprinkle red chilli powder and bhuna jeera powder on the dahi.
6. With a spoon, pour the chutney on it, in circles.
7. Garnish with bhuna jeera, red chilli powder and fresh mint (poodina).
8. Leave in the fridge for atleast ½ hour for the bread to soak the curd.
9. Serve with some hari chutney and also some extra imli chutney.

Note: Although these are not individual pieces of dahi badas, it tastes very much like dahi badas. I am positive you will like it!

Broccoli Achaari

Broccoli is extremely low in calories and a very healthy vegetable too.

Serves 4   cal/serving 40

400 gm broccoli or hari gobhi (1 medium flower)
1 tsp oil
1 tsp kalonji (onion seeds), 1 tsp rai (mustard seeds)
1½ tsp saunf (fennel seeds)
2-3 saboot lal mirch (whole red chillies)
½ tsp haldi, 1 tsp red chilli powder, ½ tsp garam masala, 1 tsp dhania
1½ tbsp sirka (vinegar)
3 tbsp tomato puree

Indian LOW FAT

1. Cut the head of broccoli and cut into small florets. Peel the thick stem.
2. Cut the peeled stem into thin round slices.
3. Heat 1 tsp oil. Add kalonji, rai, saunf and sabut lal mirch. Wait till saunf changes colour.
4. Reduce heat. Add haldi, red chilli powder, garam masala and dhania powder. Add 1 tsp salt.
5. Add tomato puree. Mix.
6. Add broccoli. Add vinegar and mix well. Lower flame and cook covered for 5-7 minutes, till crisp tender. Stir occasionally, sprinkling water in between to prevent it from scorching. Serve hot.

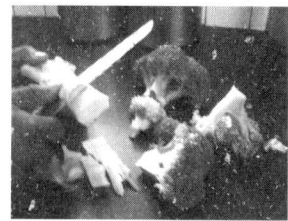

Phalli Tamatar Kairi

French Beans with green mango.

Picture on page 68 *Serves 4* *cal/serving 38*

250 gm french beans - threaded & cut diagonally into ½" pieces
1 medium kairi (unripe mango) - peeled & cut into tiny cubes
½ tbsp oil, ½ tsp rai (mustard seeds), ½ tsp kalaunji (onion seeds)
2-3 whole, dried red chillies, 4-8 curry leaves
2 tbsp chopped fresh coriander, 1 tsp salt, 3 tomatoes - cut into tiny pieces

1. Boil beans in ½ cup water & ½ tsp salt, till just tender. Do not over cook.
2. Heat ½ tbsp oil. Reduce flame. Add rai and kalaunji. Reduce flame.
3. After ½ minute add the whole red chillies and curry leaves. Stir for a few seconds.
4. Add coriander, salt and tomatoes and stir-fry for about 2-3 minutes. Add the water of the beans. Cook on high flame till it is almost dry.
5. Add the diced mango and the green beans. Stir for about 5-7 minutes.

From the Oven

Kabuli Chana Bake

Picture on facing page *Serves 6* *cal/serving 166*

2 cups kabuli chana (chick peas) - soaked overnight
¼ of red, yellow or green capsicum, for garnish

TOMATO SAUCE

1 tbsp oil, ½ tsp ajwain, 1 onion - cut into thin slices
½ kg tomatoes - blended to a puree in a mixer
3 tbsp readymade tomato puree, 2 tbsp tomato sauce
4 flakes garlic - crushed, ¼ cup chopped coriander leaves
½ tsp chilli powder, ½ tsp sugar, 1 tsp salt, or to taste

WHOLE WHEAT SAUCE (MIX TOGETHER)

1 cup milk, 2 tbsp finely chopped onion, 1 tbsp aata (wheat flour)
2-3 flakes garlic - crushed, ½ tsp salt and ¼ tsp black pepper

1. To boil Chanas, drain water from the Chanas. Add 4 cups water and 1½ tsp salt. Pressure cook to give one whistle. Keep on low heat for about 10-12 minutes. Remove from fire. Keep aside.

Indian LOW FAT

2. For the tomato sauce, heat 1 tbsp oil and add ajwain. After a minute, add onion and fry for 2-3 minutes till it slightly changes colour.
3. Add the fresh tomato puree, ready made tomato puree, tomato sauce, garlic and chopped coriander leaves. Add ½ tsp red chilli powder, ½ tsp sugar and 1 tsp salt. Cook for 10 minutes on low heat till the juice from the tomatoes evaporates and it turns slightly thick.
4. Add the boiled Chanas along with the water. Cook till the extra water evaporates and the tomato masala coats the Chanas slightly. Check salt etc. and remove from fire.
5. In a borosil dish, spread Chanas at the base of the dish.
6. For the sauce, mix all ingredients together in a pan and stir on medium heat till it turns a little thick of a saucy consistency. Spoon sauce on Chanas, leaving gaps of 2" in between. This way you get red & white strips. Start from the corner, put some sauce in a row, leave a 2" gap and then put another row to get a red & white striped look.
7. Arrange a few coloured capsicum slices diagonally on the sauce. Bake in a preheated oven for 20 minutes at 200° C. Serve hot.

◁ *Khatti Mithi Subzi : Recipe on page 57*

Tandoori Paneer ki Subzi

A delightful paneer dish which is relished with meals as a side dish.

Picture on page 57   Serves 4   cal/serving 97

250 gms paneer - cut into 1" cubes
¾ tsp salt
¼ tsp red chilli powder
1 tsp lemon juice
¼ tsp haldi (turmeric powder) or a pinch of tandoori red colour
½ tbsp oil
2 capsicums - cut into fine rings
2 onions - cut into fine rings
¼ tsp kaala namak (black salt), ¼ tsp salt
2 tsp tandoori masala

GRIND TO A ROUGH PASTE WITHOUT ANY WATER
1½" piece ginger, 2-3 green chillies
1 tsp jeera (cumin seeds), 3-4 flakes garlic - optional

Indian LOW FAT

1. Cut paneer into 1" squares, capsicums and onions into fine rings.
2. Grind garlic, ginger, jeera and green chillies to a thick rough paste. Do not add water. Keep the ginger paste aside.
3. Add salt, chilli powder and lemon juice to the paste. Add a little haldi or colour to the paste.
4. Apply ¾ of this paste nicely on all the pieces. Keep the left over paste aside.
5. Grill this paneer on a greased wire rack and grill at 180°C for 15-20 minutes or till it is dry and slightly crisp on the outside. Keep aside till serving time.
6. At serving time, heat ½ tbsp oil in a kadhai. Fry onion and capsicum rings for a few minutes till onions turn transparent.
7. Add the left over ginger paste and a few drops of lemon juice. Add kala namak and salt.
8. Add tandoori paneer pieces. Sprinkle tandoori masala. Toss for a few minutes till the paneer turns soft and is heated properly. Serve immediately.

Jeera Khumb with Baingan

Serves 6 *cal/serving 127*

200 gm mushrooms - sliced
300 gm baigan - bharte waala (1 small round brinjal) - cut into ¼" pieces
1½ tbsp oil
2 tsp jeera (cumin seeds)
1 onion - sliced thinly
2 tbsp dry bread crumbs
¼ of a tomato - deseeded and chopped

MIX TOGETHER
1 tbsp tulsi (basil leaves) or mint leaves
3 tbsp atta (whole wheat flour)
3 cups skimmed milk
1½ tsp salt, or to taste
½ tsp black pepper powder
½ tsp red chilli powder

Indian LOW FAT

1. Slice mushrooms and cut baigan into ¼" pieces
2. Preheat the oven to 180°C/325°F.
3. Mix the milk with the wheat flour gradually in a bowl, to avoid lumps. Add salt, black pepper powder, tulsi and red chilli powder. Mix well with a beater and keep aside.
4. Heat the oil, add the jeera, when it turns golden, add onions and stir fry over medium heat for a minute.
5. Add the mushrooms and baingan, stir fry over high heat for 3-4 minutes till the brinjals are half cooked.
6. Add the milk mixture, stirring constantly. Mix well. Cook stirring till the mixture turns thick.
7. Transfer to an oven proof serving dish.
8. Sprinkle the bread crumbs on top and then arrange the tomato pieces on top.
9. Bake for ½ hour before serving. Serve hot.

Step 1

Step 1

Step 7

Indian Chana Pizza

Ready-made kulchas are topped with chanas and grilled.

Serves 8   *cal/serving 63*

6 ready made kulchas
1 cup kabuli Chanas (safed channe) - soak in water overnight
1 tsp ginger-garlic paste
¾ tsp salt, ½ tsp garam masala, ½ tsp bhuna jeera powder
2 tsp Chana masala, 1½ tsp lemon juice, or to taste
1 green chilli - chopped, 2 tomatoes - chopped, 1 tbsp oil
½ cup red anaar ke dane, ½ cup poodina chutney
1 onion - cut into slices and separated into rings, 2-4 tbsp chopped coriander
some tomato sauce - to spread

1. Drain soaked Chanas. Put in a pressure cooker with 1 tsp ginger-garlic paste and 1½ cups of water. Pressure cook to give 2 whistles and keep on slow flame for 8 minutes. Remove from fire.
2. After the pressure drops, drain the Chanas. Put the cooked Chanas in

a kadhai. Add ¾ tsp salt, ½ tsp garam masala, ½ tsp bhuna jeera powder and 2 tsp Chana masala. Mix well and add lemon juice to taste. Mix the chopped green chilli and tomatoes also with the Chanas.
3. Heat 1 tbsp oil till very hot. Pour on the Chanas immediately. Mix.
4. Add ½ cup hari or poodina chutney to the Chanas. Add anaar also.
5. Spread 1 tbsp of tomato sauce on a kulcha. Spread some onion rings on it. Spread some Chanas on onions.
6. Sprinkle some more onion rings and coriander on top.
7. Grill for about 15 minutes at 180°C or till the bottom of the kulcha gets crisp. Do not over grill, it turns hard. Cut into pieces and serve.

Low Calorie Desserts

Phirni

Set phirni in earthen containers to give a special flavour to the dessert.

Serves 6 *cal/serving 62*

3½ cups (700 gm) milk
¼ cup basmati rice or rice flour
1/3 cup sugar (slightly less than ½ cup) or to taste
2 almonds (badam) - shredded, optional
2-3 green pista (pistachio) - soaked, peeled and sliced
2 small silver leaves - optional
seeds of 2-3 chhoti illaichi (green cardamom) - powdered
1 drop kewra essence or 1 tsp ruh kewra

1. Soak rice of good quality for about an hour and then grind very fine with 4 to 5 tablespoonfuls of water to a paste. (Rice flour may be used as a substitute.)

2. Dissolve the rice paste in ½ cup milk and make it thin.
3. Mix the rice paste with the remaining 3 cups milk in a heavy bottomed pan. Cook on medium heat, stirring continuously, till the mixture is of creamy consistency.
4. Add sugar and cardamom powder and stir.
5. Simmer till sugar is fully dissolved and then boil for 1 minute.
6. Remove from fire and add ruh kewra or the essence.
7. Pour the mixture into 6 small earthern containers.
8. Chill. Decorate each dish with a silver leaf and a few shredded nuts.

Note: For Fruity Phirni,
1½ -2 cups assorted fruits (melon, watermelon, green & black grapes strawberries, chikoo, apples) - chopped

1. Take 4 individual stem glasses (can use small glass bowls also). Place assorted fruits at the bottom of each glass.
2. Top with the prepared phirni. Garnish with varq and almonds. Place in the fridge till serving time.

Stuffed Khubani in Syrup

Picture on page 103 *Serves 8-10* *cal/serving 60*

13 large dried imported seedless khubani (dried apricots, orange in colour)
some rose petals, to garnish

FILLING

50 gms paneer - grated very finely
seeds of 3 chhoti illaichi - powdered
5-6 badaam (almonds) - crushed coarsely
a drop of kewra essence

SYRUP

½ cup of sugar, 1 cup of water
2-3 chhoti illaichi (green cardamoms)
2 drops of kewra essence

Indian LOW FAT

1. Take a khubani, make a small slit at one side of the khubani.
2. Insert the knife straight inside without puncturing at any side. Rotate the knife gently, creating space for filling. Let the other end be intact. Do not puncture it, otherwise the filling will come out.
3. For filling, grate paneer very finely. Add powdered illaichi seeds, crushed baadam and kewra essence. Mix gently.
4. For the syrup, heat sugar, water and illaichi together in a pan. Give 2-3 boils. Cook on low heat for 3-4 minutes. Add essence.
5. Add khubani to the syrup and let it cook for another 2-3 minutes. Remove from fire. Let it cool in the syrup.

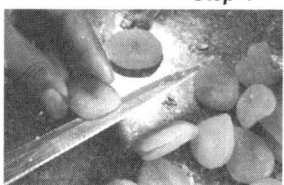

Contd...

6. Take one piece of khubani at a time. Fill atleast ½ tsp of the paneer filling in each piece. Push gently.
7. Put back in the syrup. Keep in the fridge for atleast 2-3 hours before serving for the dessert to taste good.
8. At serving time, garnish with rose petals. Serve at room temperature.

Step 6

Step 7

Indian LOW FAT

Orange Rabri

Bread is used to thicken milk. Orange rind with rabri tastes great!

cal/serving 70   *Serves 4*

1 kg toned milk, seeds of 2-3 chhoti illaichi - crushed
1 slice bread - sides removed & ground to crumbs in a mixer, 2-3 tbsp sugar
1" fresh orange peel, scrape white pith - cut into thread fine strips and chop

ORANGE TOPPING

5 gm (½ packet) agar agar (china grass) - soaked in 1 cup ready made orange juice for 15 min, 1 tbsp sugar, 1 large orange - peeled & skin removed

1. Place milk & illaichi in a kadhai. Boil. Simmer for 30 min on low heat.
2. Add fresh bread crumbs. Cook for about 10 minutes till slightly thick like rabri. Add sugar to taste. Mix and remove from heat.
3. Add orange peel. Pour rabri into a shallow serving dish. Cool till set.
4. Heat soaked agar agar on low heat, for 4-5 minutes (do not boil), till it melts completely. Remove from fire and wait for 1 minute. Pour liquid over cold rabri in the dish. Garnish with peeled orange segments.

Seb (apple) ka Meetha

Serves 8 *cal/serving 87*

2 apples - grated with the peel

SUGAR SYRUP

¼ cup sugar, ¼ cup water
seeds of 4-5 chhoti illiachi (green cardamoms) - crushed
2 drops kewra essence

KESARI MILK

3 cups milk
¼ tsp saffron (kesar)
3 tbsp sugar
1 cup milk mixed with 2 tbsp cornflour

OTHER INGRDIENTS

1 apple - grated with the peel
4-5 almonds and 4-5 kishmish - chopped
seeds of 2-3 chhoti illaichi (green cardamoms) - crushed

Indian LOW FAT

1. For the sugar syrup, put sugar, water and illaichi in a kadhai. Bring to a boil. Simmer on low heat for 2-3 minutes.
2. To the syrup, add 2 grated apples. Cook for 3-4 minutes till dry. Add kewra essence and mix well.
3. For the kesari milk, boil milk with kesar in a clean kadhai.
4. Add sugar and reduce heat. Simmer for 15 minutes till it is reduced to about ½ the quantity. Do not let it get thick.
5. Add cornflour dissolved in milk. Bring to a boil, stirring constantly. Cook for 2-3 minutes on low heat till thick.
6. Add the sweetened apples. Cook till quite thick. Remove from fire.
7. Grate 1 apple and spread a layer of grated apple at the base of a medium size serving dish.
8. Pour the apples in milk over and spread. Sprinkle some illaichi powder and chopped nuts. Keep in the fridge for 2-3 hours to set.

Chenna Kulfi

Khoya is substituted with low fat paneer.

Serves 15 *cal/serving 37*

1 kg (5 cups) skimmed milk - at room temperature
½ cup sugar
75 gm paneer - grated finely (¾ cup)
2 tbsp cornflour
seeds of 3-4 chhoti illaichi (green cardamoms) - crushed
1 tbsp kishmish (raisins), 1 tbsp shredded badam (almonds)

1. Dissolve cornflour in ¼ cup milk.
2. Heat the rest of the milk with sugar. Boil and keep on fire for about 20 minutes, till reduced to half the quantity.
3. Add illaichi & cornflour paste to the boiling milk, stirring continuously.
4. Continue boiling, by lowering the flame, for about 2-3 minutes. Cool.
5. Add paneer, kishmish and almonds. Check sugar. Remove from fire.
6. Fill in clean kulfi moulds and leave to set in the freezer for 6-8 hours.

Stuffed Khubani in Syrup: Recipe on page 96 ➢

BEST SELLERS BY Nita Mehta (Vegetarian)

- **Dinner Menus**
- **Eggless OVEN Recipes** 
- **LOW FAT Tasty Recipes** 
- **MORE DESSERTS** 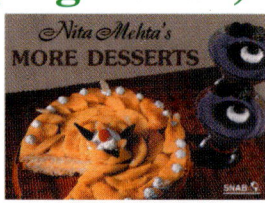
- **PRESSURE COOKING** 
- **SANDWICHES** 
- **Different ways with CHAWAAL** 
- **MUGHLAI Veg Khaana** 
- **CHINESE Veg Cuisine** 
- **SOUPS & SALADS** 
- **BREAKFAST Veg Special** 
- **Great Ideas - COOKING TIPS**